A Crow Doesn't Need A Shadow

A Guide
to Writing Poetry
From Nature

Lorraine Ferra

Illustrations by Diane Boardman

GIBBS·SMITH
→P
PUBLISHER

PEREGRINE SMITH BOOKS
SALT LAKE CITY

This is a Peregrine Smith Book, published by Gibbs Smith, Publisher, P.O. Box 667, Layton, Utah 84041

Cover and Design by Diane Boardman, Port Townsend, Washington

"Poetry Field Trips" by Lorraine Ferra was originally published in a shorter version in *Sierra,* September/October 1984, Volume 69, No. 5.

Grateful acknowledgment is made to the following for permission to reprint previously published material:

New Directions Publishing Corporation for the excerpt from "The Tulips" by Denise Levertov in *The Jacob's Ladder.* Copyright ©1961 by Denise Levertov. Reprinted by permission of New Directions Publishing Corporation.

Wordscape: A Creative Writing Journal, Winter 1987, for the excerpt from "Harvest Moon" by Don Stap. Copyright ©1987 by Don Stap. Reprinted by permission of Wordscape Publications.

Library of Congress Cataloging-in-Publication Data

Ferra, Lorraine.

A crow doesn't need a shadow : a guide to writing poetry from nature / Lorraine Ferra ; illustrations by Diane Boardman. — 1st ed.

p.   cm.

ISBN 0-87905-600-2 (pbk.) ISBN 13: 978-0-87905-600-1

1. Poetry—Authorship—Juvenile literature. 2. Nature in literature—Juvenile literature. [1. Poetry—Authorship. 2. Nature—Poetry. 3. Creative writing.] I. Boardman, Diane, ill. II. Title.

PN1059.A9F47 1994

808.1—dc20   93-34991
                                                      CIP

For the children
who wrote the poems in this book,
for their imaginative spirit
and their respect for the earth.

Contents

Open the Door
An Invitation to Readers

Over three hundred years ago, the poet Matsuo Bashō said, "To learn about a tree, go to a tree." Bashō was considering more than the scientific facts you learn about trees. He was suggesting that the creatures of the natural world speak a language, one perhaps different from yours, but one you can understand if you listen with your imagination.

The poems in these pages were written by people who know that a river "talks to you in splashy ways," or who can hear rain "reciting prayers against the windowpane." Some have stood under a sky filled with "whispering stars" or in a quiet snowfall that made the night seem "wordless." Others have watched a growing pine tree "becoming the grandfather of the animal-shaped clouds" or supposed that because of its sleek, deep darkness, "a crow doesn't need a shadow."

These writers were learning a new language by giving their full attention to the world around them. Their thoughts and poems grew naturally as they sat under a tree or followed the flight of a bird or a leaf in the wind. Like Bashō, they went out to the source.

Every chapter of this book, every poem, is a different door you can open to the natural world. Choose any one of these doors, open it, and step quietly outside with your pencil, paper, and imagination.

Poetry Field Trips

WILDFLOWERS

Everything was calm
even the blossom
with its mouth open.

Rebecca Loutensock, 8

Can you remember a summer day when you were lying on your back in cool grass, watching clouds float overhead? If they seemed more like a flock of sheep grazing in a blue meadow than clouds, you were thinking like a poet, and your thought was a poem. You were imagining like another poet who wrote about tulips

becoming wings
ears of the wind
jackrabbits rolling their eyes.

A strange idea? "Weird," you might say. But when you think about it, the common names for certain wildflowers, as "wild" as they sound,

. . .not only describe their appearance, but also make those flowers memorable. It seems they were named by poets who are always trying to see the "ordinary" things of the earth as the wonders they actually are. You can try the same sort of thing, and what you discover about the earth will be as valuable as finding a new friend.

One way to become more familiar with nature is to go on poetry field trips. These are ways of exploring the natural world by observing rocks, plants, or animals, then writing down your thoughts about them in poems.

On your first poetry field trip you might search just for a flower. Look around your yard, neighborhood, or city park. If your family is planning a weekend drive in the countryside or to the mountains, comb the terrain for wildflowers. Besides carrying a notebook and pencil, take along a field guide to help you identify the flowers by name.

Once you have chosen a flower, sit beside it for a while. What does it smell like? Are its leaves and stem smooth or fuzzy? What about its color? Is it bright or dark? Are the petals thick, delicate, velvety? What do the flower's different parts remind you of? Use your answers to these questions to write a short poem describing the flower. Here is an example written by a boy who found a wild rose growing alongside a canyon trail:

The Wild Rose

High in the silent forest
a wild rose sits. In its center
a harmless sun rests. Its petals
are wings of a baby chick.
Its leaves are hands waving
good bye.
Adam Lewis, 11

"A harmless sun" is a wonderful way to describe the flower's sun-like stamens. The writer doesn't tell us that the petals are delicate, but we know it by the way he compares them to "wings of a baby chick." At the end of the poem he hints at the wild rose's short life by depicting its leaves as "hands waving goodbye." You can almost feel the wind shaking the rose's fragile form.

Like the writer of this poem, remember that poems do not have to rhyme. Trying to find a rhyming word can sometimes ruin the idea you started out with.

After reading the next poem, look at it again. See how the writer makes comparisons in the first four lines, and then, in the last four lines, how she creates a feeling of harmony in the quiet actions of the blossom, the bird, and the flower's buds:

Ladies - Tresses

It's white and lacy
like the bottom of a gown.
The stem is the color of the sky
on the night of a hurricane.
The blossom bows its head
as a bird whistles in the wind,
And the buds come out, slowly,
as if to hear their first directions.

Cynthia Summers, 10

Here are two other poems about wildflowers:

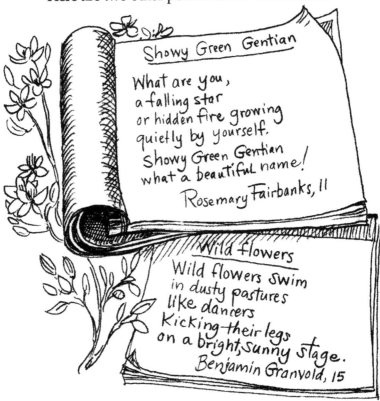

Showy Green Gentian

What are you,
a falling star
or hidden fire growing
quietly by yourself.
Showy Green Gentian
what a beautiful name!
Rosemary Fairbanks, 11

Wild flowers

Wild flowers swim
in dusty pastures
like dancers
Kicking their legs
on a bright, sunny stage.
Benjamin Granvold, 15

Notice in the poem about the gentian how the writer not only speaks *about* the flower, but also *to* it, just as she might talk with a good friend. She had never seen this wildflower before, except in a wildflower field guide, and could have written about it after looking at its picture in the book. But the tone of excitement in her poem seems to come from encountering the Showy Green Gentian alive in the mountains on a fresh spring morning.

Keep in mind that during any season of the year you can find flowers growing somewhere. In different parts of the country you can even come across small but hardy flowers poking their faces through mounds of snow or rebounding under pelts of steady rain.

And don't forget those often overlooked flowering weeds, such as dandelions, growing in lawns or sprouting through cracks in city sidewalks. Lots and fields yield many different kinds of flowers, like the thistle, whose prickly head and leaves can sharpen your imagination for writing.

After finishing your poem you might note the date and the place where you found the flower. You might also want to sketch the flower next to your poem. Gradually your notebook will grow into a diverse landscape of wildflower poems.

Wild Thistle
Feb. 11, 1992
Field behind Nick's house

spider

Weather

Thunder rattles the woods.
The legs of the storm run west.

Jenny N. Alexander, 8

Weather is an endless source of ideas for poems. You need only to step outside to feel the freshness of new-fallen snow or a light rainfall. If circumstances limit your activities and keep you indoors, a poetry field trip can be as quick as a few steps to a window. From there you can watch dark thunderclouds riding toward you like a herd of buffalo or catch sight of a rainbow before it disappears.

Think about how clouds, rainbows, snow, hail, fog, lightning, and other weather phenomena often look like other things; then write about them as if they *are* those things:

The Rainbow

What is a rainbow? Sometimes
I think it is a beautiful bracelet
that turns on a girl's wrist.

Rick Lee Robins, 7

Besides describing a weather subject being like *one* thing, write a poem which becomes a list of several things you associate with that weather. Think of doing it this way: transform your subject into

1. an animal
2. a tree or flower
3. a tool
4. a person
5. a musical instrument

You don't have to put them in that particular order, but remember to include all five categories like this:

Rain Is a Tall Thin Girl

Rain is the petals
falling off a daisy.
It is a siamese cat
walking in the fields.
It sounds like the high
key on a piano.
It is a tall thin girl.
Rain is a hammer
hitting the ground hard.

Elizabeth Bradley, 7

Notice how skillfully the writer of this poem shows the various qualities of rainfall by thinking about rain in the five suggested ways. When she describes rain as "the petals falling off a daisy," she reminds us of at least two things: the petal-like shapes of raindrops and the way rain sometimes falls lightly, almost without sound.

Visualizing rain as a cat "walking in the fields" can make us wonder about a number of things: how rain often flattens and mats down grass and weeds, or how it appears almost as a predator tracking its prey. Making the cat Siamese is perhaps the writer's way of painting in our minds the color tones of the rainy day.

Her careful writing also helps us distinguish the various sounds of rain, as suggested in the *ping* of "the high key on the piano" and the *thud* of "a hammer hitting the ground hard."

A very important feature of this poem is the writer's selection of a title. After she finished writing the poem, she decided that comparing rain to a "tall thin girl" was her favorite part. She could have called her poem simply "Rain," but her unique title arouses our curiosity and leads us to suspect this will be a very different poem about rain.

Another way to explore weather is by imagining how you would feel and what you would do if you were a streak of lightning, a patch of fog, a thunderhead, a sunbeam, or a snowflake.

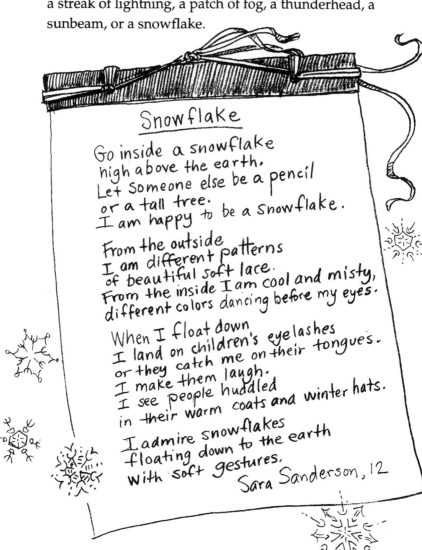

Snowflake

Go inside a snowflake
high above the earth.
Let someone else be a pencil
or a tall tree.
I am happy to be a snowflake.

From the outside
I am different patterns
of beautiful soft lace.
From the inside I am cool and misty,
different colors dancing before my eyes.

When I float down
I land on children's eyelashes
or they catch me on their tongues.
I make them laugh.
I see people huddled
in their warm coats and winter hats.

I admire snowflakes
floating down to the earth
with soft gestures.

Sara Sanderson, 12

To write a different kind of poem about weather, start by making a list of action words (verbs) that you usually associate with people. Words like

erases   yawns
swallows   weaves
recites   Kneels
carves   paints
gossips   skips
apologizes

Then, make a second list of verbs you commonly associate with different animals. Words such as

gallops   slithers
hibernates   wags
perches   laps
grazes   pounces
slinks   swarms
roosts

Next, decide upon some aspect of weather for your subject; then choose two or three verbs from each of your lists to start writing your poem. For example, if your subject is "fog," you might begin by describing how

25

fog *erases* certain objects you ordinarily see on a clear day. You might continue by telling where fog *perches* or *grazes*.

By using uncommon verbs, the boy who wrote the following poem makes us think about wind as if it were some animal-like creature:

Wind

Wind nibbles
on the walls
of buildings.
When it hunts
in the forest,
it rubs its chin
on the trees
and wipes its mouth
on their leaves.

Tyler Jeffries, 8

We often use the word *blows* to describe the action of wind. What makes this poem so captivating is the writer's choice of uncommon verbs for wind:

With these words he helps us to think and wonder about wind as something quite mysterious, especially when we read that it "rubs its chin . . . and wipes its mouth."

Search for the effects of weather around your area. While walking on a winter day, you might notice evidence of how very cold air froze swirling movements of water in a gutter or pond. During a long, hot spell following heavy rainfall, you can sometimes find patterned ripples of hardened mud in places like dry gullies. Leaves can tell stories about encounters with wind or rain. In its assorted designs on the earth, weather continually leaves clues of its activity for you to discover.

Look for animal tracks in snow, mud, or sand.
Consider shapes of icicles, fog banks, and dust devils.
Have rock formations and trees been sculpted by wind?
No matter what you might be doing——bicycling
downhill on a gusty day, or falling asleep to the rhythm
of rain on the rooftop, you are a part of the ever-
changing drama of weather. Watch it, feel it, listen to its
music, smell and taste it. Then keep a weather log of
your own calm and stormy poems.

Birds and Other Animals

Is that the oncoming darkness
or the raven in front of the sun?
Ethan Rampton, 14

Birds and their
habits provide abundant
ideas for poetry. You could fill
notebooks with poems about their
shapes and sizes, various colors,
and enchanting songs. Be on the
lookout for the different species that appear
around your home. Check your state map to see
if there is a refuge for migratory birds somewhere
nearby. Many cities have aviaries with birds you may
never find perched on the branches of trees in your
yard—birds like swans, cranes, toucans, and flamingos.
Mountains, fields, marshes, and swamps attract other
species; and there is probably a park in your town with a
pond sheltering ducks, geese, and other water birds.

You might begin writing about a bird by using a comparison method. Concentrate on different parts of the bird's body and what those parts look like. Also, think about the bird's graceful or awkward movements and about the similarities between bird behaviors and human habits. The boy who wrote the following poem about a Snowy Egret fishing in a river channel tells us something about the bird's physical appearance and also how it seems to display human pride:

The Question Mark

The Snowy Egret flaps his wings once
or twice, to show his pride. But
when a noise comes near, he pokes
his head up out of the water
like a question mark.

James Fairbanks, 9

Grace and beauty highlight the next poem written by a girl who is convinced that swans are the most remarkable birds of all:

Swans

They float like leaves over the lake,
like crowned Kings,
but different in ways—
their long necks resemble arches
that have been standing
for thousands of years.

De Ann Perkins, 12

Sometimes, if you are in the right place at the right moment, you might see an unfamiliar bird from a far-off region alight on a branch outside your window during its migratory travels. In the following poem the writer saved the moments she spent watching a Cooper's Hawk devour its prey in her backyard:

The Hawk in My Yard

The hawk comes in
on silent wings
and perches high atop
the old bare-branched tree.
His piercing beak pokes
his dead prey
and little sparrow feathers
fall to the ground.
He sits with his back to me
and, with a wary eye,
turns his head
to watch
over his shoulder,
then shifts his feet
and ruffles his feathers
as the cold night air draws near.

Allison Prescott, 12

The writer just happened to be outside when the hawk came in "on silent wings." As carefully as the hawk watches "with a wary eye," she observes every movement it makes. Her poem seems like an eyewitness account by a reporter at the scene.

Notice her precise, descriptive language: *piercing, wary, shifts, ruffles*. You can tell how important it is for her to choose the most appropriate words to describe her sudden visitor. Her last line, "as the cold night air draws near," leaves us shivering with her in the darkening yard filled with the hawk's presence.

While you are on a poetry field trip to find and write about a bird, you might be attracted by a different animal, such as a horse scratching its ear against the post of a corral:

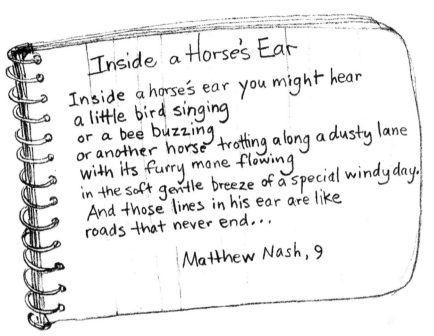

Inside a Horse's Ear

Inside a horse's ear you might hear
a little bird singing
or a bee buzzing
or another horse trotting along a dusty lane
with its furry mane flowing
in the soft gentle breeze of a special windy day.
And those lines in his ear are like
roads that never end...

Matthew Nash, 9

Perhaps you can remember a time you saw a rabbit bound across a road and disappear into a thicket of bushes at the side. Consider how a rabbit spends its day. What does it see and hear while it moves around looking for food? Make a list of those sights and sounds. Then begin a poem by writing, "Through a rabbit's eyes you will see" or "With a rabbit's ears you can hear." Include the ideas from your list.

Remember to use vivid words for the actions and appearance of the animal you are writing about. For example, in the poem about the horse, the writer does not say the horse is "running down a road." He has the horse "trotting along a dusty lane." His choices of words like *trotting, dusty,* and *lane* make his poem come to life for us and appeal to our senses: we can hear the rhythm of the horse's hooves and smell the dust rising from its tracks.

Keep in mind a particular animal's surroundings and write a poem about watching and being with that animal as it moves around its home. It could be a poem in which you speak to the animal.

The Fawn's World

Delicate fawn,
prancing down the moonlit path,
your footprints seem endless.
I hear you landing, softly,
over the crackling leaves.
Teach me to count
the rays of the winter-white moon
that glows in your eyes.
Rain dances about your hooves
as if clapping
for your performance
as you dash to your destination
under the trees.
Walking with you through
the lush, green grass,
I feel I can learn
the teachings of the world.

Richard Lo-chi Tso, 13

Wherever you live, you are sharing that space with many nonhuman creatures, and they, in turn, are sharing it with you. Acquaint yourself with the varieties of wildlife that inhabit the area. Writing about these fascinating neighbors could be your own way of celebrating their presence on this planet with you.

Building a Nature Wordscape

I'm drifting through words like snow in an hourglass.

Ali Wilson, 13

Obsidian
Newt
Swarthy
Grebe
Borealis
Balsam
Alevin
Grebe
Igneous
Yarrow
Lynx
Vole
Estuary
Conifer
Osprey
Acacia
Indigo
Bramble
Basalt
Quartz

Imagine spending an entire year among a group of friends or classmates without learning their names or anything about them. It's a silly thought. But what about that tree in your yard, or the one in your neighborhood which you pass everyday? Is it a sycamore, a maple, an elm? And the birds that perch on its limbs—are they finches, juncos, chickadees?

Becoming acquainted with nonhuman inhabitants of the earth by learning their names is a first step to discovering their habits, features, and patterns. If you know someone by name, for example, chances are you also know other things about that person. The same thing applies to your relationship with nature, and a growing nature vocabulary helps you to describe the earth's variety with precise and inviting details.

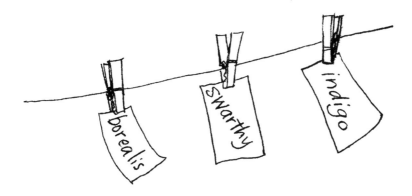

You could begin building a "nature wordscape" by using a method which the American writer Jack London devised when he decided to become a writer. Whenever he came across a word he wanted to learn and remember, he jotted it down on a scrap of paper and copied out its meanings from the dictionary. He stuffed these scraps into his pockets. He would take the words out and study them as he walked to a friend's house or went sailing on San Francisco Bay in an old boat he had bought for $6.00.

After a while, Jack strung a clothesline across his bedroom, and with clothespins attached the words to the line. Every time he crossed the room, there were the words—musical, powerful, beautiful words that he was beginning to use in his speaking and writing. Words like *primitive, estuary, ptarmigan, borealis, swarthy,* and *indigo.* Jack London drew from the store of words he learned this way to find the exact language he needed for describing his experiences around the world and in his own northern California home country. He chose to live in the Valley of the Moon—a place name that appealed to his love for appropriate words.

You can use a similar method to develop a nature vocabulary, or you can think of other ways. Here is an example of what one girl did as she began learning the names of trees in her town. First, she found a large fallen branch of a white oak tree and brought it into her room. Then she walked around her neighborhood with a tree field guide, thumbing through it until she could identify many different trees.

Next, she outlined the shapes of the various trees' leaves on construction paper and cut out the shapes. Then, on each paper leaf shape, she wrote the name of the tree with

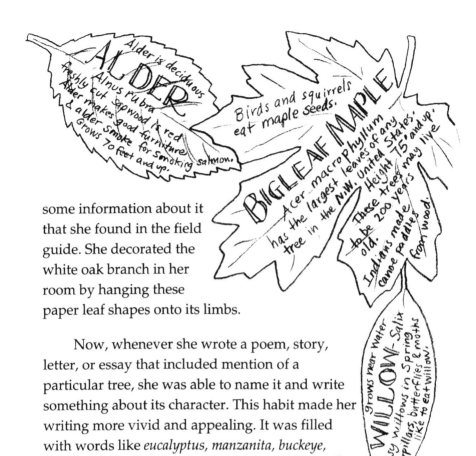

some information about it that she found in the field guide. She decorated the white oak branch in her room by hanging these paper leaf shapes onto its limbs.

Now, whenever she wrote a poem, story, letter, or essay that included mention of a particular tree, she was able to name it and write something about its character. This habit made her writing more vivid and appealing. It was filled with words like *eucalyptus, manzanita, buckeye, catalpa, ginkgo, cottonwood,* and many other colorful names.

By learning the names and features of trees and writing about them, she developed her knowledge and appreciation of the tree kingdom around her. Also, the information from her field guide prepared her to watch for certain characteristics of different trees at varying times of the year. She began noticing, for example, how the star-shaped leaves of the sweetgum glisten like a galaxy after a rainfall. She learned how the sycamore gradually creates a patchwork quilt around its branches and trunk through a lifelong process of bark peeling.

Besides a tree vocabulary, you could also build a bird, mammal, flower, fish, sky, pond, or weather vocabulary, using an idea like the girl's project with the fallen branch. You might construct a mobile or design a wall mural for your words. Or, like Jack London, you could use a clothesline. Better still, invent your own way of building a nature vocabulary.

Pacific Giant Salamander - eats mice and gartersnakes. Makes sounds like a rattle.

Shooting Star pink

Indian Paintbrush red-orange

White Catchfly flower light pink. sticky stem!

Bleeding Heart (Red)

White furry Cat's-ears with yellow circle

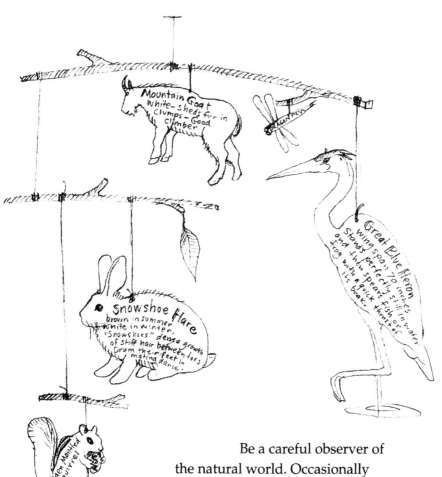

Mountain Goat
White- sheds fur in
clumps - Good
climber

Snowshoe Hare
brown in summer,
white in winter.
"Snowshoes" dense growth
of stiff hair between toes
Drum their feet in
mating dance.

Golden Mantled Squirrel

Great Blue Heron
wing span 70 inches
Stands perfectly still in water
and they spear fish or
frog with a quick thrust of
its beak.

Be a careful observer of the natural world. Occasionally check out nature field guides from your city or school library. Be sure to catch nature documentaries on television. And, always, watch and listen for descriptive words and names for the earth's inhabitants and features. Learn these words and names until they are as familiar to you as your closest friends. Then use them in your writing. Soon you will find that everything you write will reflect the diversity of the world you live in.

Keeping a Nature Journal

Being lazy in the meadow.
It is like placing my head
on a pillow of wind, rivers,
and dreams.

Ben Burns, 8

Listening and Listing

One March morning when winter was turning to spring, a boy was awakened by what he thought was the sound of children chasing each other around the side of the house. When he pulled back the bedroom curtains, he found the real source of the sound: huge, heavy icicles, which had hung all winter like glistening knives from the eaves, were melting in the warming air and dripping into their own small puddles beneath his window.

He got back into bed to listen to the icicles' winter-spring music. He closed his eyes and thought of similar sounds: salmon slapping their tails and fins in the river; the clapping of small stones in the surf on the shore; and pine needles ticking in the high winds in the woods.

He reached for a journal which he always kept with him and listed these impressions. Then he added:

Because he wanted to keep an account of nature's daily happenings, he recorded the date, March 16, closed the journal, and lay back on his pillow, eyes closed, listening.

You could begin keeping a creative nature journal with a simple listening and listing experience. Good listening times can be in the early morning or evening when your thoughts might not be interrupted by traffic noises or the screams of children playing. First, choose a place outdoors where you like to be alone. You could hide in the reeds near a pond, climb a favorite tree to a comfortable, sturdy branch, sit on the edge of a playground, or lie back in the grass in your yard.

Let's say you choose to sit by a
pond. Think about living in the
pond and being dependent on it for your survival. If
you approach the pond thinking that way, your senses
will be very sharp. Be as alert and quiet as a mother
duck guarding her eggs in the tangles of cattails and
ferns. You will know you are ready to detect the
slightest movement or sound if you can hear your own
steady breathing.

If you wish, close your eyes and just listen for a
while. You don't need to be concerned about listing
sounds in your journal right away. Spend time enjoying
and wondering about them. Give your attention to the
variety of bird songs, the buzzing and droning of
insects, and the rustlings of grasses and reeds.

You might be startled by a sudden splashing of water. Could it be the leaping of a frog, a turtle, or a fish? Or perhaps even a muskrat or a beaver? Maybe it is a heron fishing for pickerel.

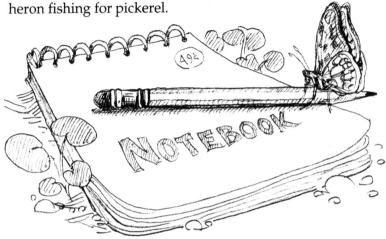

When you feel ready to write, start listing some sounds. Then, like the boy who wrote about icicles, think about other things that make similar sounds and create your own comparisons. Could the twittering of swallows darting for caddis flies over the surface of the water seem like aspen leaves chattering in an autumn wind? Or could a garter snake moving through cord grass sound like sand rippling over a desert dune?

In your journal, make a list of the actual sounds you hear on the left side of the page. On the right side, list your comparisons for those sounds. You could even select your favorite sound and comparison and use them to write a short poem. Here is a poem written by a girl who compared the paddling of ducks to the sound of raindrops:

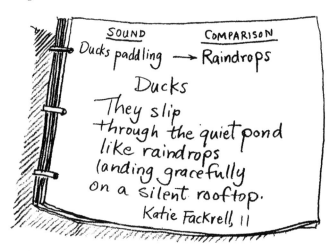

SOUND   COMPARISON
Ducks paddling ⟶ Raindrops

Ducks
They slip
through the quiet pond
like raindrops
landing gracefully
on a silent rooftop.
Katie Fackrell, 11

Because this writer was listening carefully, she was able to create a visual image as well as a sound image in her poem. This is an important fact about listening: if you can become very quiet, your other senses will sharpen too. Your stillness will become an invitation to the natural world to show you some of its secrets. A cricket frog might jump onto your leg, mistaking it for a log; or a swallowtail might alight in your hair, thinking it to be a tuft of wild grass.

Time after time, and in unexpected ways, nature will reward your careful attention.

Backyard Explorations

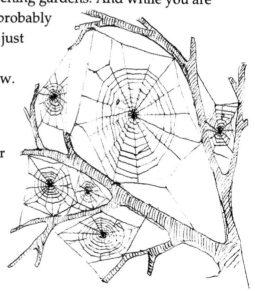

Your own yard and neighborhood can be the best places for exploring nature's activity, even if you live in a big city. Great Horned Owls are often seen roosting on roofs and steeples as well as in trees; falcons and hawks are known to nest on ledges of skyscrapers; raccoons find their way to ripening gardens. And while you are asleep, spiders are probably spinning their webs just outside—or maybe inside—your window.

Look around outside in the morning sunlight for the spiders' elegant natural designs. If the sun and air currents are just right, you might catch sight of one or several of these "little trampolines" waving in the breeze on taut strands. Check for the orb weaver in the center and for whatever prey is still caught in the silky trap.

Morning is a good time to find an abundance of other natural wonders. If you have a cat, follow it on its first prowl of the day. Watch how the cat concentrates totally on something as small as a ladybug climbing a blade of grass. Try to be as aware as the cat; that kind of attention will help you to observe and to write.

If you become interested in something but are not sure about how to start writing, you could begin by writing an acrostic. One form of an acrostic is a poem in which you write the name of something in capital letters going vertically down the left side of your journal page. Then you start building a poem about the subject with words that begin with each letter. Here is an example:

S trands of a harp
P ulling the dew from the sun
I n the middle of a summer
D awn,
E ntering through a gate of string
R iding upon air.

W hen the wind rises, it looks like a flag,
E legant as a hand-sewn quilt
B lowing in the breeze.
Scott Burrell, 15

The next poem is another example of an acrostic by a girl observing clusters of lilacs in her neighborhood:

Lovely is the
Inspirational and
Lackadaisical lilac. The sweet smell and
Ahhh of a purple haze
Cascading among a field of wonders.
Ryka Melnyczenko, 14

Since the first word of each line has to start with a particular letter, the acrostic form can inspire you to discover new possibilities in your subject as you go from line to line. The letter at the beginning of each line directs your imagination in surprising ways. If you cannot decide what to write about, try writing an acrostic using your name. Then let the letters of your name help you to focus on the variety of things around you.

Here is an example of a personal name acrostic:

Brown moss creeping over the maple tree
Rapid winds whispering
Everywhere life
Egg-shaped insects hatching like new chickens
Many flies around me like bees in a hive
Under every leaf a new surprise
Running sunlight through the trees
Plenty of grass to give homes for grasshoppers
Hidden mud under the rocks
Yawning after a full day
Bree Murphy, 12

Your name acrostic can be a personal way of seeing yourself in the natural world. It can also remind you of how you and so many different things live together in unique relationships on the earth.

A Night Sky Journal

No matter where you are, the sky is always above you, playing out its daily drama with the sun and moon, stars, clouds, and changing colors. Consider the sky at night with its constellations and different phases of the moon. In 1851 the great American naturalist, Henry David Thoreau, realized how often we allow the moon to pass, night after night, without paying any attention to its beauty and mystery. "One moon gone by unnoticed," he wrote. Imagine what you miss by not looking for each night's moon and its changes in shapes and brightness. Years and years of moons!

Watch for the harvest moon during the autumnal equinox in late September. This colorful full moon was originally named because it appeared at harvest time and shone so brightly that farmers could work late into the night harvesting their crops. A poet once described this moon as "a pumpkin-colored elephant skipping rope." His vivid comparison is almost as exciting as the moon itself.

You could record the appearances of the moon each night in your journal by creating comparisons. Could the crescent moon be the "wind-filled sail of a pirate's ship," or the "tip of a giant's toenail"? What about the half-moon? Can you imagine it being the "hull of a rowboat sinking into a vast black lake"? Picture the full moon. Is it a "clock without hands" or a "cantaloupe growing in a field of dead weeds"?

Here is a poem by a girl who looked back through her journal, selected her own favorite comparisons for the crescent moon, then put them together as a poem:

What is the Crescent Moon?

Is it the sly eye of a sleek black cat
poised to pounce on its prey,

or the crust of a pepperoni pizza
Sneakily eaten by a child?

Is it the streak of fire following a
Shiny black Porsche
racing to catch up with the sun,

or one of many ships
lost in the mysterious Bermuda Triangle?

Is it a slit in the sky
allowing spirits to enter the atmosphere,

or the most precious jewel
in the raven-black hair of night?

Jana Farr, 13

You could also follow a similar procedure focusing on the stars and their constellations or on the formations of clouds rimmed by starlight or glowing from moonlight. Think of writing about the moon in your journal and sketching it each night for an entire season or for a whole year. What a wealth of appreciation you will develop about our closest neighbor in space!

A worthwhile practice to establish while keeping your nature journal is noting the location and date of each of your journal entries. This is especially useful if you often return to the same spot for observation and writing. Observing nature's activity in the same place throughout the four seasons will sharpen your awareness of the natural world. You will learn when certain species of animals leave and return to the area, the life cycles of various wildflowers, grasses, and trees, and the impact of different kinds of weather.

A unique kind of history, a natural history, is happening around you every moment of the day and night. If you pay attention, use your imagination, and take your journal everywhere you go, you will always be ready to record it.

Other Explorations

Every place, creature, or event in the natural world provides an opportunity for wondering and writing. The next nine sections offer new ideas for continuing to fill your journal with poems about your observations. Each experience starts with one poem followed by some thoughts, questions, and suggested observing and writing activities to help you discover other parts of nature. The questions will encourage you to go deeper into the poems and into the mystery and beauty of the natural world which the poems explore. Think of these questions and experiences as new paths you can walk on alone or sometimes with a friend who can exchange different feelings on a shared journey.

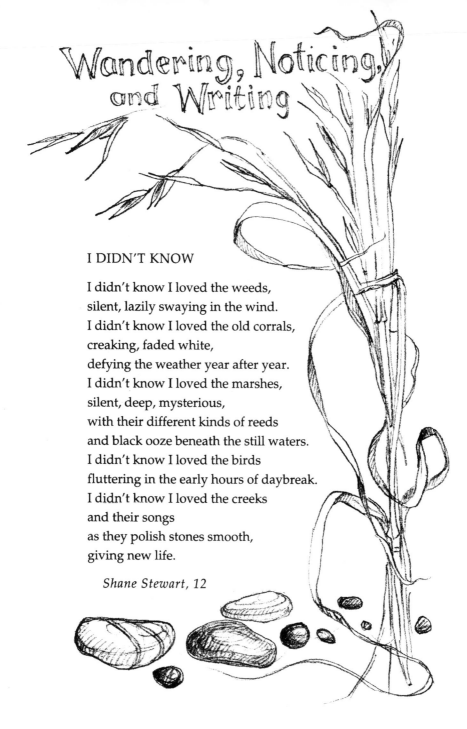

Wandering, Noticing, and Writing

I DIDN'T KNOW

I didn't know I loved the weeds,
silent, lazily swaying in the wind.
I didn't know I loved the old corrals,
creaking, faded white,
defying the weather year after year.
I didn't know I loved the marshes,
silent, deep, mysterious,
with their different kinds of reeds
and black ooze beneath the still waters.
I didn't know I loved the birds
fluttering in the early hours of daybreak.
I didn't know I loved the creeks
and their songs
as they polish stones smooth,
giving new life.

Shane Stewart, 12

We often become so busy in our routine of activities, that we hardly notice what surrounds us every day. Shane's title, "I Didn't Know," and the way he repeats it several times in the poem suggest that he is experiencing familiar sights, sounds, and places as if he were discovering them for the first time. His "rediscovery" of creeks, weeds, and weathered corrals moves him to write about them with a feeling of deep joy.

Questions and Thoughts to Explore

What are some things in your yard or neighborhood that you haven't spent time looking at for a while?

What is one of the most beautiful sights you experience when looking out a window at home, school, or another place you visit often?

What kinds of weather or animal sounds do you hear when waking up in the morning or falling asleep at night?

Even though Shane mentions many things in his poem, he actually focuses on only six:

1. weeds

2. old corrals

3. marshes

4. birds

5. creeks

6. the creeks' songs

Because his description is so rich and full, we are able to experience much more. For example, he doesn't merely tell us, "I didn't know I loved the marshes." He describes the marshes as "silent, deep, mysterious, with their different kinds of reeds and black ooze beneath the still waters." What other parts of his poem are filled with such vivid details?

Read the poem aloud. Which part do you like the sound of best? Does reading it aloud help you to experience the marshes, for example, as if you were there?

Choose a word you like in this poem. Say it aloud. Think about how the sound of the word makes you feel. Does it make you feel restless, lonely, contented, jittery, peaceful?

Who or what, in your opinion, is being given "new life" at the end of Shane's poem? What do you think he means by "new life"?

Suggestions For Writing

Carry your journal around your neighborhood. Stop occasionally and use your senses to experience what's around you. Kneel and look closely at a blade of grass or patterns in the dirt. Notice smells. Is someone baking bread somewhere, or is a breeze carrying the scent of a certain flower? Walk up to a tree and smell the trunk. Say the word *trunk* aloud.

Jot down your observations every so often. Then listen for a few minutes and compare human-made sounds, such as car traffic, with bird songs or the rustling of leaves. Look around and watch the ways that shadows of trees, fences, or buildings sketch themselves on sidewalks, streets, yards, or fields.

Using your notes, begin a poem listing and describing these "ordinary" things as if you had just discovered them.

Finding a Companion in Nature

I WANT TO BRING THE WIND

I want to bring the wind
wherever I go
so I won't be lonely.
When I ride my yellow bike
right behind me is the wind,
and when the moon shines on the sea
the wind blows my boat far.
It rattles at the windows
and knocks at the door,
but when I open it
no one is there.

Janna Fikkan, 8

Sometimes you discover something so wonderful in nature that you feel like being with it most of the time, like a good friend. During times you are without the company of friends or family, nature is with you in one way or another. It could be a single leafless tree outside your window, a wide-open sky, or a chorus of crickets in dark grass. In her poem, Janna reminds us of the companionship we can find with something in the natural world. For her it isn't something tangible, like a rock or a flower or an animal; it is the activity of the wind.

Questions and Thoughts to Explore

Which line in Janna's poem suggests to you that she considers the wind to be a friend she needs?

What part of the poem helps you feel the wind against your body?

Recall a time in a particular place when you felt a gentle or a strong wind. Describe the details of your surroundings. What do you remember seeing, smelling, or hearing? Did the wind seem to make the colors in that place weave together in different ways?

In the last four lines of Janna's poem, does the wind seem like a playful friend, a mysterious visitor, or something else?

If you could choose a kind of weather as a companion, what would it be: snow, sunshine, fog, lightning, thunder, rain, or maybe hail?

 Suggestions For Writing

Choose something in the natural world that you could consider as a companion. It doesn't have to be weather, as in Janna's poem. It could be anything: a season, an animal, a creek, a patch of violets, or the song of a bird. Exploring your yard or neighborhood could help you focus and select.

After choosing your companion, think about its different characteristics: is it bold, radiant, patient, secretive? List words that describe its different qualities.

Also, include words that indicate how it is like and unlike one of your best friends. Use some of these words in your poem.

You could begin your poem, as Janna started hers, by telling why you want your subject to be a companion that is always with you. Then briefly describe two or three things that might happen when you are together. Most likely your poem will turn into an unpredictable adventure with a remarkable friend.

Creating a Landscape

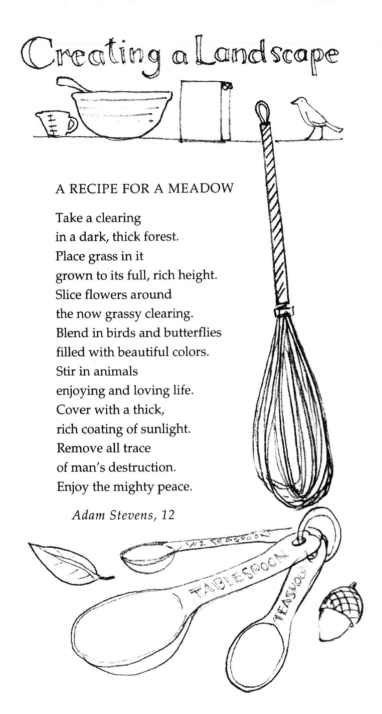

A RECIPE FOR A MEADOW

Take a clearing
in a dark, thick forest.
Place grass in it
grown to its full, rich height.
Slice flowers around
the now grassy clearing.
Blend in birds and butterflies
filled with beautiful colors.
Stir in animals
enjoying and loving life.
Cover with a thick,
rich coating of sunlight.
Remove all trace
of man's destruction.
Enjoy the mighty peace.

Adam Stevens, 12

In "A Recipe for a Meadow," Adam imagines a place where all creatures live in harmony. He uses verbs he found while thumbing through a cookbook. Just as a chef might give directions for preparing and cooking a tasty dish, Adam tells how to create a portrait of an ideal meadow. If you listed the recipe-sounding verbs in his poem, your list would look like this: *take, place, slice, blend, stir, cover, remove,* and *enjoy.*

 Questions and Thoughts to Explore

Notice the way Adam gradually develops his poem, starting with "a clearing." The clearing seems like a clean, empty bowl a cook would use to mix the particular ingredients. What are the ingredients Adam places in his container, the clearing? Can you think of other ingredients that might have been included in this meadow recipe?

Which ingredients appeal to your senses most clearly in this poem? Which of your senses is affected most when Adam says, "Cover with a thick, rich coating of sunlight"? Does more than one of your senses respond to this image?

Which different species of birds, butterflies, and other animals do you see or hear in Adam's meadow? What specific flowers do you smell and see?

What do you think about when you read, "Remove all trace of man's destruction"?

How can peace be mighty? How would you "Enjoy the mighty peace"?

 Suggestions For Writing

Look through a cookbook. As you read the directions for several different recipes, write down the verbs which tell you what to do with the ingredients. Make a list of about ten or twelve different verbs. Keep in mind that you probably won't use all the verbs you find. Be selective for your poem.

Some possible subjects might be a recipe for a cave, a foggy morning, a bird refuge, a season or particular month, a moonlit field, a river, or a sunset. Once you decide on your subject, start listing some ingredients. Let's say your poem is going to be a recipe for a hike. Besides the more obvious ingredients, such as a mountain trail and a backpack, think about including feelings related to a hike. You might enjoy the hike with something like "the companionship of a September breeze in the birches," for example.

Now—enjoy your writing!

Becoming Your Surroundings

MY MANY THOUGHTS IN THE MOUNTAINS

I am the brilliant sun
gazing at a solemn rock in the shade.
I am the cloud-covered sky
stretching like elastic
over old pines touched lightly
with soft snow frost.
I am the dark purple shadow
cast by a spruce reaching to the tip
of a tall musical mountain
snow-capped and looking over
the deep valley beyond.
I am a young girl in a red dress
sprung with blue roses.

Marian Partee, 9

In "My Many Thoughts in the Mountains" Marian offers us vivid details of what she experienced when she allowed herself to become totally absorbed in her environment. Her poem seems to be written by someone lost in a dreamy thoughtfulness of the beauty around her. She expresses her awe, not merely through description, but also through the feeling of *becoming* her surroundings.

Questions and Thoughts to Explore

Besides the obvious sections that invite your sense of sight, find parts of the poem that call upon your other senses. For example, can you hear the trees being "touched lightly with soft snow frost"?

How can a mountain be musical?

Name about three different times you have heard music not created by humans or human-made things. Think about the music of water, animals, branches rubbing together, or rocks rolling down a slope.

Recall where you were when you heard nature's various kinds of music, and compare those sounds to the sounds of human-made musical instruments.

Which parts of Marian's poem create for you a feeling of deep silence?

What do you think it is about her surroundings that makes her feel so much a part of them?

Notice how Marian portrays herself and what she is wearing at the end of the poem. Does her red dress "sprung with blue roses" make her seem as if she, too, is growing from the earth like the trees?

Suggestions For Writing

With your journal in hand, find a place where you can feel comfortably alone with your thoughts. You could prop yourself against a tree or lie back in the grass and daydream.

Put yourself in a kind of mind-wandering mood, and allow your thoughts to drift from one thing to another, like a bee alighting for a moment on one flower before floating off to the next.

Then focus your attention on something in particular—something close by, like a twig, or off in the distance, like a cloud. Concentrate on its color, texture, shape, and other qualities. Imagine how it would feel to *be* what you are observing.

You could write your poem about being one or several things. Create four or five sentences about your subject or subjects, as if you *really are* what you are writing about. Remember to fill your poem with descriptive details.

You could end your poem by describing yourself in such a way that you seem to blend in with your surroundings. Perhaps something you are wearing is the color of the bark or leaves of a nearby tree. Or maybe your hair is waving like grass in a breeze. Writing about how you resemble other things in nature can inspire you to think about your relationship to them. It can also help you to remember that you, too, are a part of the natural world.

Colors in the Natural World

ORANGE

Is it what you find
when you dig
into that
ball of mold
under your bed?
Is it the sun
as it gets ready
for bed?
Is it the hood
of an Oriole, a Tanager, the
rusty cape of a Grosbeak,
or is it clay
baked
in the scorching
desert sun,
a smashed pumpkin at
the end of October,
or the campfire
lighting the peace
of the forest?

Timothy Bosen, 11

The natural world is filled, not only with many different colors, but also with many shades and tones of those colors. Some colors are more prominent in certain kinds of weather or during specific seasons. "Orange" is a poem listing a variety of things associated with the color in several places and at various times.

Questions and Thoughts to Explore

Where in Timothy's poem do you find the color orange to be brightest?

What do you think is the "ball of mold"?

Why do you suppose Timothy wrote his poem in the form of questions? How could the poem change your responses if it were in the form of statements?

Notice where Timothy uses attractive, descriptive words. For example, instead of writing the "head" of an Oriole, he chooses the word, "hood." Find another place where his choice of words attracts your interest.

Do you think that Timothy might have looked through a bird field guide to find some interesting names of birds that are orange or have orange features?

Does placing the word "baked" on a line by itself give you a particular feeling about the clay?

Has the poem helped you to experience the color orange in a new way? How?

 Suggestions For Writing

Look around for different colors. Choose one color you see. It might be gray, if the day is foggy, or you might choose blue after catching sight of that flash of color from the flight of a damselfly.

When you decide upon a color, begin writing down the names of things around you which have that color. Also, allow your memory to recall animals, flowers, or other creatures that would be present in other seasons. You could also look through nature field guides for names to add to your list.

Besides listing what you can see, include feelings also. For example, if you choose the color purple, can you think of a feeling that seems purple? When Timothy connects orange to "the campfire lighting the peace of the forest," he associates orange not only with the orange-colored flames of the fire, but also with a feeling of calm and tranquility.

Now, review your list, and be selective. Choose about seven or eight things from your list and start building a poem about your color by describing those objects in an unusual way. Remember to fill your color poem with variety.

Dreaming Up A Place

A PLACE I KNOW

Illusions drift before my eyes.
A hand with many fingers
chases me to a land
with gnarled trees.
I linger in the path
before I climb a tree
and sit on a branch.
Hidden by leaves
I gaze hungrily at the sky,
feeding myself with the clouds,
the taste better than juicy red apples.
I touch the moist leaves
and float back to
a place I know and love.

Melissa Marsh, 11

"A Place I Know" is a dreamlike poem about an imaginary place. It is the kind of poem which can be written by first experiencing a real place in the natural world. Melissa, for example, was inspired to write her poem after climbing and sitting in a favorite tree.

 Questions and Thoughts to Explore

Which word or line in the poem gives you the first clue that Melissa is writing about a place she visited in her imagination?

Which lines really develop the poem's dreamlike quality?

What are Melissa's feelings about this place? Which words or parts of the poem express those feelings?

What prompts Melissa to "gaze hungrily at the sky"? Do you think she is hungry for food, or for something else? How can clouds "taste better than juicy red apples"?

There is one color word in the poem. What other colors are present but not mentioned?

Do you think the "moist leaves" Melissa touches are the leaves of a real or an imaginary tree?

What do you suppose causes her to "float back" from her dream?

Suggestions For Writing

Find a favorite spot outside and sit quietly for a while. A tree would be good to dream in, or you could lie on your back and wonder about the cloud shapes and colors drifting high above you. Wherever you choose to be, allow what is actually there—sounds, smells, tastes, textures, sights—to carry you to an imaginary place.

Think of it as a region where you are the only human visitor. Describe its geographical and other physical features. Is it like a hidden gully surrounded by trees, or the top of a skyscraper that pokes through the clouds? Are there mountains and valleys with rivers of rainbows? Are there grasses that grow unusually high? Is the ground bare and dry with hardy desert plants? What species of animals inhabit or visit this area? How did you get there? By hiking, sailing, flying, riding a bicycle?

Begin writing a poem, briefly describing your journey and the place you find. Mention one or two things you might do there. Help your readers feel as if they are gazing at everything through your eyes and with your excitement over your discovery.

At the end of your poem, you might tell how your thoughts returned from this dreamed-up place. Did the fragrance of flowers, the warmth of sunshine, the call of a bird bring you back?

Read your poem aloud and note how many of its dreamlike images connect in some way to your actual surroundings. The more you observe and write, the more you will see how the landscape nourishes your imagination.

Nature in Your Hand

ICE

A numbing cold sweeps up my hand like a frost-bitten storm. I try to ignore the chilling cold reminding me of its icy presence. Suddenly, my hand seems to meld into the ice, then the transparent, icy sparkle slowly and steadily rises up my body; and the lasting feeling of a chilling cold overcomes me. And in my mind I'm frozen in time, and eternity gives me its knowledge.

Hold the ice. Touch it. And feel its silence.

Nicolaas Bodkin, 11

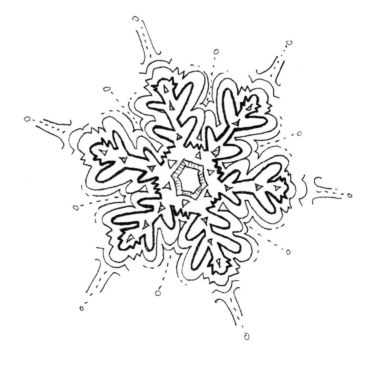

"Ice" is an example of a prose poem. A prose poem might be thought of as a brief description of an object, an experience, or a place, including an intense feeling about the subject. Although this applies to other poems also, an obvious difference is that prose poems are not deliberately broken up into specific lines.

Even writers of prose poems have difficulty explaining why they write a poem in the form of prose. Perhaps one reasonable explanation is that a writer chooses the prose form because it seems to fit the subject of the poem, just as someone chooses a particular style of clothing because it seems to fit the wearer.

 Questions and Thoughts to Explore

What do you suppose was Nicolaas' experience behind this poem? Do you think he was cross-country skiing, holding an icicle, ice fishing, or doing something else? Find places in his poem to support your idea.

Have you ever felt "a numbing cold" that affected your body "like a frost-bitten storm"?

What do you think Nicolaas means when he writes, "in my mind I'm frozen in time"?

At the end of his poem he invites us to "Hold the ice. Touch it. And feel its silence." How can you *feel* silence? Describe the silence of ice. Compare the silence of ice with the silence of something else, like a pencil, a poppy, or an old boot.

Suggestions For Writing

Write a short prose poem portraying what happens when you hold a certain object. For example, you could search outside for something like a stone or a pine cone slightly smaller than your hand. Sit quietly for a while, holding it in one hand. Close your eyes and feel its shape and texture. Hold it until it reminds you of something else. Does it rest in your hand like a boat anchored in a cool, calm lake?

Describe what it seems to become in your hand. (For Nicolaas, the ice seems to become a silent storm.) Then think about the feeling that holding it gives you. Is it a feeling of comfort, darkness, peace, loneliness? Somewhere in your poem you might want to invite your readers to taste or hear or touch that feeling.

Remember to keep your prose poem brief. If you include too many details, it will lose its focus. Keep only those details that describe the transformation of the object as it seems to become something else while you are holding it.

Rhythms in the World And in Words

SUNLIGHT

sleeps on the backs of cows
sleeps on the maple leaves in autumn
sleeps on the petals of poppies in the park

sleeps behind the moon during a solar eclipse
sleeps behind clouds in a foggy sky
sleeps behind a hill at the end of the day

sleeps on a rabbit's hole in the morning
sleeps on a dragonfly's wings
sleeps on my flights of fancy

Michelle Menne, 10

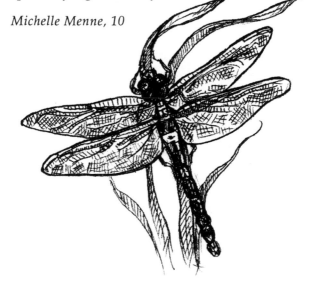

In her poem, "Sunlight," Michelle uses an uncommon word to describe the action of the sun. Her choice of the verb "sleeps" instead of "shines," the repetition of the word, and the variety of things she has the sunlight sleeping on or behind, draw immediate attention to her subject. Besides creating a feeling of the sun's widespread influence and presence, the repetition builds a sense of rhythm and flowing sound patterns from one line to the next. If you read the poem aloud, you can hear the rhythm and feel the flow.

 Questions and Thoughts to Explore

Which lines do you feel are the most rhythmic?

Why do you think Michelle chose "sleeps" to portray what sunlight is doing in her poem? What could have inspired her to talk about sunlight as sleepy? How can sunlight seem to sleep on anything?

Does repeating the word "sleeps" contribute to an overall sleepy atmosphere in the poem?

What is the most sleepy image, for you, in the poem? Which line do you feel creates an intense feeling of the sunlight's warmth?

In some of the poem's images, sunlight is sleeping on things that are moving. Where do you find those moving images of sunlight?

Can you visualize the patterns on the dragonfly's wings as sunlight sleeps on them and filters through them?

Notice how Michelle ends her poem with flying images of a "dragonfly's wings" and her "flights of fancy." Does her choice of placing those two lines together and at the end seem to bring her poem to a satisfying completion for you?

Suggestions For Writing

Choose one subject from your environment, a subject such as the grass, the sky, a river, trees, or snow. Then give it an uncommon action. For example, if you decide to write about snow, make your key action word (verb) one like "blossoms" instead of "falls."

Proceed to build a poem by using that verb for your subject at the beginning of each line. Repeating the verb at the beginning of every line intensifies the feeling of your subject's action throughout the poem. Let your title be the name of the subject, and avoid mentioning the title word in your poem.

Create a different image in each line. Notice, for example, how Michelle has sunlight sleeping on or behind a variety of things; each of her nine lines contains a new image.

Besides creating a new image in every line, include phrases that tell when, where, or how your subject is performing the action you have given it. Such details provide precise, vivid description.

You could write many lines and then go back and cut out some that might not contribute to the poem's variety or its rhythm. Read your poem aloud several times before making any cuts.

Write your poem in such a way that you and your readers can feel totally surrounded by your subject. Then share it with someone by reading it as a poem praising and celebrating nature.

Growing a Poem Naturally

NIGHT

The world's children	children
are lost in their dreams	dreams
of gentle	gentle
breezes. Darkness circles	circles
the cloudless	cloudless
sky, beneath	beneath
the whispering	whispers
stars. Young travelers	travelers
are lost in a lonely	lonely
sleep as cold as winter.	winter

Jeffrey Odell, 10

"Night" is the kind of poem you can write with a word list and without knowing before you begin what your subject will be. Before discussing how Jeffrey compiled and used his list to write his poem, let's wonder about the poem itself.

Questions and Thoughts to Explore

Who do you think are "the world's children"? Who are the "young travelers"? Could they be something other than people? Could they be leaves, animals, snowflakes?

What do you suppose Jeffrey means when he describes the children and the travelers as "lost"?

What could the children's "dreams of gentle breezes" be? Do you think of them as real breezes, or as something else?

How can stars whisper? Describe a sky in which stars seem to whisper.

How can sleep be "lonely" and "as cold as winter"?

Find a word in "Night" which describes your feelings while reading the poem.

Suggestions
For Writing

After sitting or walking outside and observing your surroundings, make up a list of ten words. Write these words in a vertical position on the right side of your journal page. Allow the place and the time to inspire your word list. Include words that tell what you see and hear and that describe the way you feel and where you are. Your last word could be the season of the year or the weather.

Next, begin writing a poem of ten lines. The last word in each line should be the word from your list. For example, notice that the first word in Jeffrey's list is "children." See how he ended the first line in his poem with that word. His second word is "dreams"; therefore, "dreams" is the last word in his second line. Notice that he changed the form of the seventh word, "whispers," to "whispering." Depending on the way your poem is growing, and if you think it is necessary, you can change the form of any word in your list.

Check Jeffrey's poem carefully to make sure you know how to proceed. Don't spend a lot of time getting started. You don't even have to think about a subject before you write. Let your poem grow line by line, and the subject, or subjects, will grow naturally as you go along.

Writing a poem this way is like walking down a path with ten curves. After going around each curve on a path, you are able to see what was hidden from your view before you turned. In your poem, the end-word of each line is a curve that leads your mind to turn and discover something waiting for your imagination.

When you finish writing, read your poem aloud. You will most likely be surprised by what you wrote. Creative writing and nature are very much alike: they lead to endless discoveries.

It seems fitting that the word, *anthology*, which is a "collection" of poems, comes from a word that means "gathering flowers." In much the same way that certain flowers grow in specific climates and places, these poems have grown out of the different landscapes and imaginations of the writers. They celebrate the world of animals, seasons, weather, trees, places, feelings, and flowers. Like flowers, with their varied colors, textures, and smells of the earth, they have been gathered here for you to enjoy and to inspire you to write about the landscape in which you live and dream.

IN A SNOWY FIELD

April . . . something has tracked across the snow,
something not concerned with lost footsteps.

It is like a snake that splits
and leaves its skin in the sand.

It is like rocks on the shore
scraped smooth by the sea.

It is like children, watching
from car windows, their house grow smaller.

Dead leaves crumble on the snow's surface,
then blow away over the elms.

Kelly Shreeve, 16

WALKING IN WINTER

I love to walk in late December
in the first fury
of winter's wrath
in the swirling snow.
It settles on my cold coat
and my breath turns
into white wandering winds
like a train trudging
through the mountains in the morning—
my white winter dreams. . . .

Keith Bateman, 14

THUNDER

Thunder is a crow cawing softly
to a tree. It is my mother
calling me in for lunch
when I was having a good time.
Thunder is a loud trumpet
playing a song I hate!
It is a black-eyed Susan.
Thunder is a screwdriver
tightening the sun to the sky.

Kristen Fikkan, 7

SAYING "THUNDER" ALOUD

I can feel the rolling madness
of darkness,
strong and unrelenting
as its mysterious syllables
move my tongue in lines of grey.

Ali Wilson, 13

STORM

While the dogwood tree
barked in the wind
and the tiger lilies ran
on the pillows of the sky
like the speed of light,
your tears fell
down your face like
raindrops falling in puddles.

Tyra Landis, 9

RED WAGON

All morning rain plunges
from swollen clouds
wearing black coats,
reciting prayers
against the windowpane.

This afternoon,
outside, rainbows gather
in a red wagon.

Stacey Miller, 16

DANDELION

Dancing around the garden
Almost laughing,
Nagging the drab
Depressed grass to be
Excited for spring.
Little sunlight,
I plant you in paper cups
On my windowsill
Near the sky.

Elizabeth Helsby, 15

HEDGEHOG PRICKLY POPPY

living under the midnight light,
embracing the ground,
feeling the silk leaves,
passionate.

Casey Stott, 11

LILY OF THE VALLEY

Little flowers
In my mother's garden
Living under the rhododendrons
Your little leaves popping up among the weeds

Oh, as fragile as glass
Fragrant as grandmother's perfume

Tulip-like leaves that fool the eye
How they blend with the grass,
Ever persistent, against the dandelions

Vehemently growing
A bell tower of white
Lightly chiming in the spring breeze
Lovingly stroking the soil with your
Energetic roots
Your precious flowers fall

Sara Lingafelter, 14

THE BIG PINE

A big pine
standing with many quills.
Are you the home
of the porcupines?

The pine
becoming the grandfather
of the animal-shaped clouds.

The north wind
making the pine shatter.

Some quills fall, landing
on a bear's paw,
making him growl.

Zachary Gertsch, 8

SHADOWS

In a sunny day
in a park
the only things that move
are black, crowded, bumping
shadows.

The shadows follow me
wherever I go like
eagles in a sky.
The shadows are
stiff, but people
move and fly.

A crow doesn't
need a shadow
because of its
color.

When I die,
the shadow
cries with me.

Jason Growler, 12

AN EARLY MORNING STROLL

They run with majestic beauty
through fields of grass,
through the pasture
shadowed by willows,
over the young tufts.

They graze all day
sampling the green plants,
nuzzling in their roots.
Two Indian ponies
happy behind a fence
under the early morning light.

Ben Gregg, 13

LOOKING INTO A HORSE'S EYES

Looking into a horse's eyes
is like going inside a cave of questions
without answers.

Scott A. Nelson, 8

THE TURTLE'S SHELL

The turtle's shell
is a sidewalk of shadows.

The inside is a
pocket of happiness.

The turtle lives
in that forest of quietness.

Justin Dickman, 8

BEES

In swift dark clouds
they travel,
carrying closely guarded
secrets, their soft humming
lost along the way.

Annie Beddoes, 13

WHEN THE FROG CALLS

at twilight
from the swamp near the birches,
I'll go to meet him
in the ooze
to swim
among the creatures
of the marsh.

We'll do the frog paddle
as the moon rises
and the stars come out—
as if from nowhere.

Then we'll jump
into a tree
and spend the night.
While crickets click
and toads croak,
we'll watch the stars,
in stillness.

And before the sun begins to rise,
we'll say goodbye
with one last dive,

swimming swiftly and smoothly
as the crickets hush
their nightly song.

Mindy Hanson, 14

A CRICKET'S EYE

I look into
a cricket's eye
and see
a falling star
in back of me.

Yolanda Adakai, 7

ELEGANT

A weeping willow
in the dreary rain,

a swan reaching
a wonderland of blue,

a tulip awaking
to a sun full of mysteries,

a starry sky
without a moon,

clear creek water
drifting down my throat
on a raft of deep red.

Vanessa Johnson, 9

A MORNING VALLEY

Ripples cross a pond.
Water drips from the ceiling
of a hollow
cave, a little river
trickling down, lacing
the valley. Wildflowers
burst elegantly.
A duck and her young
go drifting through the pond.
The valley is eternal, little
voices whispering
down through the forest.

Noah Michel, 12

INSIDE THE WOODS

I love to explore inside the woods
studded with small,
small things to think of,
and in majestic mountains,
to fly my feasting eyes,
and on ridges I root
to find studded stones
smothered in moss;
fleeting, I find
lakes like glistening eyes,
lovely, staring lonely
into the cyan skies.

Joseph Rienstra, 12

AUTUMN

Autumn—
fierce tiger,
fire of colors,
whirlwind of emotions,
a girl walking
through the woods,
wind in her hair.
Autumn—
a sheet of music
covered with
a frenzy of dots,
a beast cut loose
now free.

Stacie Greenhalgh, 15

MOUNTAIN LION

Through the broad distance
of the mountainous forest
the sleek beast drifts
like a shadow,
until it spots its prey.
Its eyes become flames
as it moves like soft music,
hunting alone
under the infinite
expanse of the sky.

Micah Ownbey, 13

THE DEER

I watched quietly as it crossed
the lonely road and wandered
into the meadow of flowers
where thick grass grew wildly.
One more appeared, then another.
They walked, peacefully,
drifting into the wind's music,
then nestled down to dream
in the silence of the flowered fields.

Emily Bosen, 14

A STORY IN THE SNOW

My cat's eyes stare into the deep
darkness as he walks along the path,
his silky, gray
fur shining in the winter coldness.
Suddenly the sun shines
radiantly on the pines,
slowly rising,
my cat continuing quietly,
his gentle footsteps
echoing his story
in the fresh, white snow.

Tia Austin, 13

SNOW HILL

The gentle wind
hovers over our house
in the small
valley. Wolves are howling
by the barn over
the hill covered in snow.
The sky is black
as horses trot
in the wordless
night.

Erik Roth, 12

NIGHT

Night swallows the sunlight
and devours the day.
It lingers across the plains
cradling the moon and stars
in its hands.

Richie Browder, 8

NIGHT

Night,
blackbird of forgiveness,
mango of memory,
pasturing on the sidewalk.
A boy with wavy black hair
is swimming through the waves of the sea.
Night,
glass of forgiveness
falling and crashing on the floor.

Nicholas Lopez, 9

ISLAND

Out of the water, the island
rises like an animal, blinking
the mist from its eyes in solitude.
The crest of this icy
mountain is the sail
of a long-lost boat, wind-polished
by breezes that have come
and gone forever. Drifting
on the sea, lost and frozen,
haunted forever by voices
that are not heard.

Tiffani Barnhurst, 15

IN MY HANDS

In my hands
there are edged rivers
as still
as the evening sun,
weeping as they continue
through this enormous journey
through stone mountains.

Christopher DeWeese, 10

MORE THAN A RIVER

Enjoying the river is the point.
Gazing at the river,
walking down the curving path,
watching it glide right by
like the tail of a kite
moving back and forth
in the sky.
Trees sway near the river,
birds sleep quietly,
not a single sound until morning.
The river is a friend.
It talks to you
in splashy ways.

John Satini, 11

THE SILVER RIVER

Among the nightfall
lies a silver river
winding
through the illusions
of clouds.
You can hear its melody
occasionally
moving toward
the nests of
your imagination.

Jason Lashua, 11

SKY POET

I am
a sky poet
writing poems
in my house
of clouds.
The birds
are carrying
my poems
in the misty clouds.

Elisa Blackgoat, 12

A Note To Educators

Learning, an eclectic mix of what we bring to an experience and the consequential change and growth, is at the core of *A Crow Doesn't Need A Shadow*. This book, grounded in meaningful language-based learning theory, is an excellent resource for teaching language arts, enhancing science studies, and advocating ecological awareness. Guiding participants toward knowledge that is connected to their lives, it extends into the broader base of a child's education and promotes metacognition—learning about how we learn.

A Crow Doesn't Need A Shadow focuses on the integration of our inner and outer landscapes. Through nature field trips, children *and* adults are invited to reflect on their personal place in the world. The book develops an imaginative clarity in which we can feel our harmony with the rhythms of the earth.

Lorraine Ferra takes us on a lifetime field trip, and we have the opportunity to develop a reverence for nature and language in their entirety. This is not a book that tells us to *use* nature as inspiration for writing or as a jumping-off point to discover ourselves. It is a book about landscape and language, about looking, listening, touching, and talking. The author and the children's poems transport us, and, with or without field experience, we are there. Our visits to meadows, ponds, or our own yards are filled with enthusiasm for life which helps us absorb our environment, share our writing, and open our senses to new ways of thinking about our world.

There are many ways to use *A Crow Doesn't Need A Shadow*. It is a field guide to take outdoors and use in silence, listening while we allow the earth to feed our imaginations. It is a field guide to study and talk about, a handbook taking us *beyond* identification of what we discover, helping us understand the wholeness of our lives.

It is also a book to use indoors—at school, at home, on vacation. We can read a chapter, then go outside to search for pinecones or icicles and examine them, holding them in our palms, perceiving their uniqueness. When we begin to respond in writing, our words come out of the immediacy of these experiences.

We can also use this book to create our own personal field trips. Encouraged by our reading, our curiosity, our need to set out on our own, we can discover a pace, delight in a place.

Years of working with students as a poet-in-residence have given Lorraine Ferra an unusual ability to help us expand our awareness. The poems in the chapters and those included in the anthology are extraordinary. When Nicholas Lopez says night is a "blackbird of forgiveness," we see it. When Melissa Marsh says, "I gaze hungrily at the sky, feeding myself with the clouds," we know it can happen. The unmistakable call of the quail, the feathered remnants of a wren's nest, the first flight of a fledgling robin are all ways we can discover our own voices, our own homes, and our own new journeys.

I have long awaited the publication of this book. It can be shared by adults and children. Take it outdoors and listen.

Mona Hirschi Daniels, Ph.D.
Department of Curriculum and Teaching
Hunter College, New York City

Acknowledgments

My thanks:

First of all to the children in Utah, Washington, and Delaware, who wrote poems with me in almost every imaginable place; their companionship and spontaneity filled my days.

And to Rosalyn Norris, fifth grade teacher at Uintah Elementary in Salt Lake City, who gathered ten-year-olds for the first neighborhood field trips and helped get the outdoor writing projects underway; my friends at the Utah Arts Council—G. Barnes, Tay Haines, Sue Heath, Jean Irwin, and Gabriella Lewon, whose encouragement and belief in this process supported my efforts.

To Nancy Ebert and Peggy Wright of the Delaware State Arts Council, Wesner Stack and Ed Schaefer, principals in the Cape Henlopen School District, and research scientist, Douglas Hicks, who arranged for a two-month residency during which I directed poetry field trips in Lewes, Delaware; Joyce Kelen, who spread the news and was always there with friendship and wise counsel; Leslie Kelen, for insightful perceptions and years of encouragement and loyalty; Stephen Ruffus, who made numerous connections for me throughout Utah; Dr. A. U. Daniels, whose generosity provided me with time and a place to work on this book; Phil Sullivan, Professor of English at the University of Utah, for his belief in my work and the immeasurable impact his teaching and friendship have made on it; Heather E. B. Brunjes, Instructor in Reading and Writing Methods courses at the University of Utah, for many years of personal and professional encouragement; Marjorie Coombs, Principal at Rowland Hall-St. Mark's Middle School in Salt Lake City, for her wisdom, accuracy, and dependable support.

To Tom Schmid, Assistant Professor of English at the University of Texas at El Paso, for his good humor and fellowship on the trails during the early poetry field trips; Kristine Kaufman, for years of friendship and wise, practical advice concerning the manuscript; Tom Bird, for his company in the canyons and his photo documentation of the field trips; Bruce Hucko, for the opportunity of working with the children on the Utah Navajo Reservation; Bonnie Oettli, educator at Hopi Elementary in Phoenix, whose teaching makes nature and nurture synonymous, for her friendship and careful reading of the manuscript.

To Carol Jane Bangs, Director of Literature Programs at Centrum in Port Townsend, Washington, for making connections for me in my new home; Chris Jones, educator and director of special programs in the Port Townsend School District, for the opportunities she has given me to work with eager children; Marty Mead, senior English teacher at Port Townsend High School, for inviting me to work with her students, for her availability to my questions about grammar and syntax, and for her steadfast friendship.

To the directors of the Port Townsend Marine Science Center—Frank D'Amore, Judy Friesem, and Anne Murphy—for what they taught me about marine biology during the miles we walked, waded, and wrote with children in the marine science summer camps.

To Phyllis Ennes, Director of the Cultural Education Program, for opening many doors for me in the Anacortes School District in Washington, for the gifts of her personal and professional support and inspiration.

To the educators I've worked with, whose dedication continues to inspire me—Lois Cook, Gretchen Dietz, Karen Durrant, Mary Gesiki, Marillyn Johnson, Dr. Larry Jensen, Carol Kranes, Carol Lee, Ron Petersen, Jan Peterson, Ann Sasich, and Barbara Webster.

To the poets whose poems I read to the children and which influenced the writing of some poems in this book directly or indirectly— Robert Mezey, my first teacher, for his passion for the art of poetry and for his poems, "An Evening" and "The doe standing poised"; Robert Bly for "A Hollow Tree" and his translations of Bashō's "The sea grows dark" and Issa's "I look into a dragonfly's eye"; John Haines for "If the Owl Calls Again," "Prayer to the Snowy Owl," and "Wolves"; Donald Hall for "Names of Horses"; Randy Blasing and Mutlu Konuk for their translation of Nazim Hikmet's "Things I Didn't Know I Loved"; Jane Kenyon for "April Chores" and "Dark Morning: Snow"; Denise Levertov for "Come Into Animal Presence," "The Breathing," and "The Tulips"; Mary Oliver for "Looking For Snakes," "Sleeping in the Forest," and "The Fawn"; Linda Pastan for "The Dogwoods"; Charles Simic for "Stone"; Gary Snyder for "As For Poets"; Wallace Stevens for "Thirteen Ways of Looking at a Blackbird" and "Vacancy in the Park"; James Wright for "A Blessing," "March," and "Saying Dante Aloud"; and Sandra Hoben, for her friendship, many hours of shared poems, insights, and walks in Little Cottonwood Canyon, and for her poems, "New Moon" and "What the Night Left Behind."

My thanks to the following for permission to reprint previously published material: *The Port Townsend Jefferson County Leader*; the San Juan School District in Blanding, Utah, for poems from *A House of Clouds: Children's Poems from the Utah Navajo Reservation*; and the Utah Arts Council for poems originally appearing in state anthologies.

My special thanks

To Diane Boardman, whose illustrations and design transformed the manuscript into a wonderful book; for what she taught me about glacial geology; and for the lilies that mysteriously appeared in my yard after her report of the passage of a shadowless crow.

To Naomi Clark, who gave many hours to reading the manuscript and offering suggestions during the last weeks of her life. Because of her, this is a better book than it would have been.

To Mona Hirschi Daniels, for providing comfort of the heart and hearth, for her active presence in the field trip program and the manuscript from the beginning, for the use of poems written under her direction, for unswerving loyalty.

To Richard Harmston, whose reflective nature and hours of patient listening and advice have contributed greatly to this work.

To Catherine Smith, my editor, for risking on uncharted ground and for her sensitive readings of the manuscript in its various stages. I owe much to her insistence on clarity.

To Don Stap, who introduced me to Bear River Bird Refuge and yellowheaded blackbirds, and taught me how to call up pine siskins; whose steady, clear thinking was, at all times, only a letter or a phone number away.

And finally, to Jean Tarascio, whose years of faith, friendship, and penetrating insights have helped to build the backbone of this work and for the use of poems written through her instruction; for incalculable hours of listening, reading, and editing. Her eye and ear for the integrity of language are present everywhere in this book.

Lorraine Ferra
Port Townsend, Washington
1993

Author Presentations

Lorraine Ferra works with the Poets-in-Residence
programs of several states.

She also gives presentations and workshops
on the uses and adaptations of this book.

If you would be interested in arranging a workshop
presentation or a residency, please contact the publisher
or write to the author at
Wordscape, P.O. Box 93,
Port Townsend, Washington 98368.

Made in the USA
Charleston, SC
19 June 2011